TALE IN VERSE

POEMS OF DIFFERENT COLOURS OF EMOTIONS AND STORIES OF LIFE.

NIRA NAGARAJAN

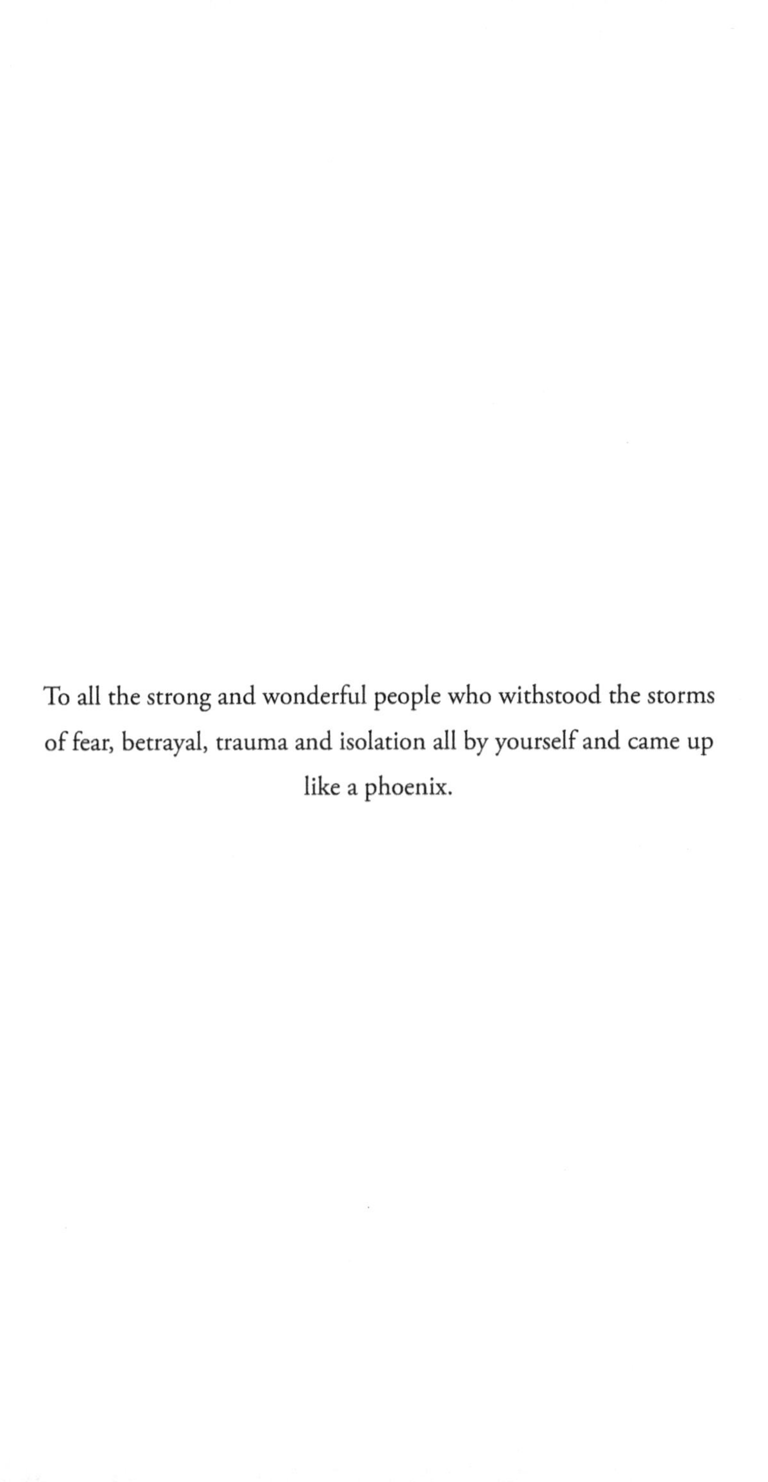

To all the strong and wonderful people who withstood the storms of fear, betrayal, trauma and isolation all by yourself and came up like a phoenix.

Contents

Contents

Preface

Life is never same for everyone. Situations aren't constant. When the destiny takes unexpected turns in life, emotions starts to washout. As an unexpected rainstorm. And they make our life into a palatte of colours, mixing and separating them. Every emotions that overtakes brings us up and down just like the rollercoaster. Overcoming or staying back in that situation is where our life diverts.

If the darkness has stolen the light and you can't find after trying, then bring up yourself as the brightest light.

There are 30 poems in total in this book which was written for six years. When I had fallen to the depths of emotions and hardships, books and words were my greatest support.

Creating tales that are expressed in verses is what I brought into light from the darkness of within to shine bright.

This book is already published in my Wattpad page @talks_by_nira

- Nira Nagarajan

Acknowledgements

My whole journey through the life was never easy and without these wonderful people, my dreams wouldn't have come true. Firstly, I've to thank Notion Press for giving me this wonderful oppertunity for making my biggest dream come true. Then I would like to thank my sisters by heart, Ganga.Pradeep and Sruthi.S . They understood my callibre and stood by my side throughout my journey, as the biggest support. They were the best critics as well as the best promoters. My family and friends who encouraged me in my dreams to come true. Emotionally, they stood my side in the storms of my life throughout this journey.

I can never forget Dr.Aiswaryalakshmi.M, my teacher who supported and helped me whole-heartedly getting my work published and meeting me with Ms. Ahla Iqbal *(Author of Twenty Is Winter)*. Thank you Ahla chechi for supporting me and introducing me here.

The wonderful readers and well-wishers who had always supported me in Wattpad and Instagram for my creations can never be slipped out of my mind. I'm highly obliged for your support.

"" Even in the darkness of eyes, a blind person can sense the light of life,

not through their vision, but with the hold on to faith and hope.""

1. The Girl

Walking through the woods I saw her, standing apart -
And staring...
It was very very dark.
No one was about I was lonely there,
But for her in that spot with brown hair and blue eyes,
with tears awash,
Hesitant to speak, with a face bleak -
Holding a candle.
But alas!
It was a dream -
A realisation of loneliness,
A hint of Sadness,
Deep in my heart.

2. The Redamancy

• 2 •

The wave of the ocean-
Kisses the feet,
Staying beside you-
Fingering our arms,
The breeze embraces-
As our eyes meet,
I see our life in
Which isn't easy,
But is as beautiful as you.

3. Silence

The sky falls -
As the dawn,
The splashes touch the ground -
As the dark crowd,
Blocking the light -
As the world might,
The vision turns to night-
Vanishing the stars.
Thunder crumbles the soil -
As lightning burns the foil,
The world screams hard -
Restricting the voice,
The trembles of land -
With anger in the tide,
Ending the live -
Living the hive.

4. The Shell of Bow

• 4 •

As the feet falls on sand-
Leaving the mark on land,
The bed of water tides-
When the crab hides.
The sky in blue-
With the patch of cloud,
As the birds flew-
From the waves in loud.
Sitting on the shore,
Looking into the light,
Touching the sand-
As the waves hide and seek,
A shell came up-
When the wave left bank,
The shine bow glare-
With the fall of light,
Brought a bright in dark-
Inside the mind.

5. Meraki

The heart flips -
As the eyes knots,
Something flying inside the tum,
The blood rushes-
All over cheek,
As the hand stretches-
With a rose of might.
The lip stretches-
Into the most beautiful smile,
The cold hands touches the green,
Feeling the chopped thorns,
"The wine is sweet -
But not as you",
The words slashed my drums-
But in the heart, it gums.
The blue sky -
Drew the bow in mine,
The view in Eiffel -
Made the bit bright.

6. The Candour

Thé Sun sets down-
As the tear falls down,
The beat stops -
As the trust strips,
You were the sun-
That set with false.
The sky come dawn -
As the tear falls down,
The beat strikes the crown,
As I became the sun-
which flourished on candour.

7. Mine

Walking through the streets,
All alone at midday-
Thinking about the past;
I heard a bark beside me,
A cute but sad one.
Lookin' there I found two little eyes-
Whose body is bathed in mud,
His look into my eyes was so piercing -
Asking some help,
Asking some love,
Asking some care.
I took him home-
N' cleaned him up;
His happiness n' naughtiness -
Became my world.
His barks, his licks and cuddles -
Became my love.
His understanding and care-
Became my universe.
He was none other than the puppy -
Covered in mud,
He is my baby-
Source of peace.

He is my Mine!

8. Hunters of light

The breeze feels cool
As the sun spool
Even the warmth
Brings a horror
An unknown silence
Of an unknown beginning
That has the terror-
Of ripping the soul.
Changes around -
Gets the chill high,
Every facts turning to myth-
As the cuckoo does to crow,
The world glorifies in the palter-
The smirks over them brighter.
The clouds get dark-
As the thunder forms,
The beats races -
With vacuumed container,
The shadows of the hunter:
The hunters of light -
Falls on the land,
Trembling the Earth.

9. Field of Lily

Over the way-
Under the blue sky,
Breathing the smell-
Near the bell;
The field of lily-
Dancing in may,
Feeling the petals-
Over the tips,
Feet touching the ground -
Goes to the depths of the soul,
The sun bathes-
As the cold breeze tides.

10. Until I Met You

The day was breezed,
As the sun shined
Down across the street,
Playing with dandelion-
In the floating leaves,
Up and down-
With countless laughs.
The eyes got stuck-
Skipping a beat,
Can the apple be as red-
As my cheeks,
The lips felt dry-
As the breath rose.
There stood in black-
With Rolex on,
The shoe shined-
As the carbonados,
The hair flipped back-
Making the best-made.
The moment I fell-
Out of the world,
The eyes were laid -
Making the shiver,

The steps made close-
As my legs were numb.
The life was beautiful,
Until I met you.
As the eyes laid,
Turing it peace.

11. Day I Get

The scar was starry-
As the sky,
From the depth of the ocean -
To the flow in veins,
The vision was blurred -
As the dark over-powered,
From the day I met-
Till the day I get.

12. The Lost Light

The day became dark,
The dawn has fallen down,
The light has become memory;
The light which was along-
Has been lost on the way.
Were we the reason to lose it?
Don't know.
All we know is that -
We have loved them more than enough -
N' now we have lost.
Falling into the black hole -
Where it'll never come back,
But the hope for its return-
Is all in heart.
As it's our best in heart..

13. Blood Turned Black

The way she entered the world,
The trust overflowed -
With Love over spread,
The healer in blood_
Swindle by dubbed.
Healed stamped on-
Over the cure,
Breaking her trust-
Inducing hate,
Demolishing heal,
As the blood turned black.

14. There was a Romeo, There was a Juliet

There was a Romeo,

There was a Juliet,

Whom known as -

The idol of love;

Travelling through the train -

All alone with their book,

Came a stranger -

The talk was impressive,

The way was genuine -

Soon the bud of friendship bloomed.

Grown through ages,

There came quakes,

There came storm,

There came laughs,

There came cries,

There came fights,

There came confessions -

And a new story.

There was a Romeo,

There was a Juliet,

Whom known as -

The idol of love;

But we were different,
We were unique,
We drew a new painting of love-
with love, understanding,
fight, Sorrow,
Trust and Lust.
We drew a love story,
Where we are the idol of love.

15. Smile

With the fallen blindfolds,
Witnessed the world of dark and hate,
Killing every innocence -
And stabbing the heart.
Her wound turned scar_
And mind in war,
All she hides-
In the smile of tides.

16. The Tyndall

The bird sings-
As the wind hits,
Opening the eyes-
Into the dark,
A lark sitting beside-
Bringing a shine in heart.
Not so long she stayed,
As she vanished -
There entered a Tyndall,
Hitting my vision -
To bring the bright.

17. Everything is Right-While nothing feels Right

Boiling on sand-
While chilling in waves,
Walking over -
While swimming across,
Bruises drips-
While bleeds float
Everything is right,
While nothing feels right.
Breathing of air-
While gurgling of water,
Clapping of hands -
While flapping of fins,
Wandering gets stalked-
While stalking gets wandered,
Everything is right -
While nothing feels right.
Heights of green -
While depths of blue,
Birth of sun-
While submerge of sun,
Flourish of colours -
While mysteries in colours,

Everything feels right -
While nothing feels right.

18. Lurk of Light

Nothing feels right -
In the lurk of night,
The aches of heart -
Masked in smile.
Never knew the cycle -
Of life was a loop,
The whole world of fire-
Burning the tire.
The tears are controlled -
As the world mocks,
"We warned you before -
They'll never stay."
The fight for ones-
Who never felt one.
Nothing feels right-
In the lurk of night,
Loneliness embraces-
When the truth hits back,
The hope of trust -
Shattered to dust.
The one's who-
Were the greatest gift,
Set back the check-

Of never the same for them.

19. The Aching Heart

Closing the eyes deep,
Falling a drop of rain _
From the left eye,
The memories of laughs,
The memories of promises,
The memories of laughs,
The memories of hugs,
The memories of support.
Comes in front as phases,
Your words than then and now-
Are echoing in my ear,
Aching in my heart.
Know that time changes-
The lives but,
Could it change the feel for each other,
Don't know
But all I know is that -
Missing the old you.

20. The Death And Time

Time was a miracle to all,
All loved her -
And adored her beauty.
Death was dark and fear,
All hated him-
For his duty.
When all ran behind the Time,
She fell for the death,
And the legend began.
Astoned by this-
The world stood still,
As their love taught the world -
Love and Trust.
They worked dutifully,
For the world beautifully-
Past, Present 'nd Future.
They wedded each other,
Ignoring the forbidden thoughts -
Spilled by the whorl,
Spreading love.
Their love was blessed-
With three beautiful triplets,
They filled the world with-

Memories, Life 'nd Hope.
When past enjoyed memories,
Present focused on current time-
And future played with the upcoming.
They filled the world with -
Understanding, Love 'nd Hope.
And taught the world-
Death is a duty,
Not hatred.

21. The Night @ Nine

A drop of water fall on mine -
At night at nine,
As the eyes dropped one,
There came a heavy breeze-
As I sobbed,
There came two hands-
Promising forever.

22. Vibrant Of Light

The blossom of vibrant -
Purities of life,
From the pain falls alone-
To heal raises along,
The dark world -
Filling the charm of hope;
The warms of chest-
Along the wraps around -
With inseparable lips,
The blossom of vibrant -
Peace of life,
From the bows of one-
To the heads for us,
The bullying world -
Turns chittering silence-
As the spread of charismatic light.

23. Lost Soul

Wandering through the woods,
As the life's flow would,
The day gets brighter-
As it hair gets lighter,
The swollen eyes -
With the rolling droplets,
Heavier the pace feels-
As the breath fades.
Nothing feels the self,
As of the soul is lost,
Tripping near the bank
Facing the reflection in the cold,
The brightness around darkens-
Getting filled with black.
The grass turns thorns -
As the petals dry off,
Piercing into the skin-
With silent screams,
The drops are exhausted-
As the heart falls.
Blurring the vision-
'nd wounding the skin,
Tripping into the lake-

Pulled into the depths-
Of an unknown place.

24. The Red Eyes

Walking through the buzz,
Under the clouds -
Of bewildered light;
The red eyes falls,
As the pace races.
Over the heights of might,
Getting the lava-
Ready to pour;
The red eyes falls,
As the pace races.
Swallowing the light,
Pourin' the blood -
'nd flooding the gloom;
The red eyes falls,
As the pace races.

25. Searching of Light

The flustered wind-
With shivering leaves,
The tremble of rock-
In the fear of storm,
That tears to bleed-
But not to end.
The rats sinks in-
As the vision goes dark,
The unknown known-
To the prey of dark,
Running in pace -
With the fear of dawn;
Searching the light.
The wet cold paws -
With uneven breaths,
The pit of hell-
Preparing torment.

26. Ours, Not Only

Death seems to be easier than live, My love.
Death seems to be easier than live;
Until the life is ours, Only our self -
And not the reason for others life-
To live.
Tears seems to be easier than laugh, My love.
Tears seems to be easier than laugh;
Until the tears is ours, Only our self -
And not for the one who taught you laugh-
In tears.
Pain seems to be easier than peace, My love.
Pain seems to be easier than peace;
Until the pain is ours, Only our self -
And not to watch the one who gave you peace-
In pain.

27. Changes to Light

The scar brightens -
Along the time hightens,
Memories marked in -
The bruise of thin,
Falls of night-
Lessons to might,
The rightful to righteous,
With the fears of dark -
Changes to light,
And the greed for life,
Changes to die.

28. Baby

The breeze hits
As the eyes opens,
A wave of love
Down on the knees,
The rose comes forward-
As the tear falls.
The vision of breeze
Pulls back the time,
The feel of love
The feel of betrayal
Fills the heart -
By seeing the apologetic face.
The hatred is overcome-
By the touch of a paw,
Those eyes never showed betrayal -
But love,
The best thing ever in my life,
My baby!
The licks of kisses,
The cuddles of hugs,
Makes me feel-
The best person.

He made me strong.
He made me grow.
Looking back at the rose,
I bid the final good bye -
With my baby,
The world full of support
As the breeze embraced.

29. The Espresso

Stepping through the green -
Under the blue,
The breeze felt free,
The water felt calm,
The tentacles of grass-
Tickling the under toes,
Lyin' on it-
Felt the embrace.
Opening the eyes-
Tears falls,
Hit the truth-
Of broken wings.
A cold wind touched,
The magic of love-
Cured the wound.
The whistle of trees-
Soothes as it sings,
The blooming flower-
Filled me a self-lover.

30. Whorl of Light

Walking through the path –
Of the world's cycle,
Changes forbidden-
With the rule of myth.
World runs for -
Power, fame, money,
Never wishes for the truth-
And live for the myth.
The difference in beings-
Gets some guts,
Searching and bringing light-
Out of dark.
They starts to break
The power of rule,
And spreads out the light-
To the whorl.